Broadway Christian Church Fort W...
Letter of Unity
Hook, Martha

P9-DBT-515

0000 2453

LETTER OF UNITY

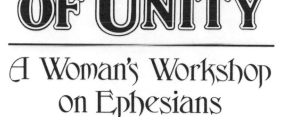

A Woman's Workshop on Ephesians

STUDENT'S MANUAL

Martha Hook

Lamplighter Books Grand Rapids, Michigan
Zondervan Publishing House

PROPERTY OF
BROADWAY CHRISTIAN CHURCH LIBRARY
910 BROADWAY
FORT WAYNE, IN 46802

Letter of Unity: A Woman's Workshop on Ephesians
Copyright © 1986 by Martha Hook

Lamplighter Books is an imprint of Zondervan Publishing House,
1415 Lake Drive, S.E., Grand Rapids, Michigan 49506.

Library of Congress Cataloging in Publication Data

Hook, Martha.
    Letter of unity.

    "Lamplighter books."
    1. Bible. N.T. Ephesians—Text-books. I. Title.
BS2695.5.H66   1986   227'.5'0076   86-18982
ISBN 0-310-26191-0

All Scripture quotations, unless otherwise noted, are taken from the HOLY BIBLE:
NEW INTERNATIONAL VERSION (North American Edition). Copyright © 1973,
1978, 1984, by the International Bible Society. Used by permission of Zondervan
Bible Publishers.

All rights reserved. No part of this publication may be reproduced, stored in a
retrieval system, or transmitted in any form or by any means—electronic,
mechanical, photocopy, recording, or any other—except for brief quotations in
printed reviews, without the prior permission of the publisher.

Edited by Pamela M. Hartung

Printed in the United States of America

        87   88   89   90   91   92 /   / 10   9   8   7   6   5   4   3   2   1

CONTENTS

ACKNOWLEDGMENTS

This study on Ephesians has not been just a writing project; rather, it has grown as small groups in several places have studied the book with me and with my husband, Phil. The actual concept of using a relational approach to the book began as we ministered to a group of couples at a weekend conference where Phil was the speaker. This book, then, is the pooled effort of all of those classes, where I have learned far more than I have taught. I give my deepest thanks to Phil for his encouragement to put our project in print for women and to my lifelong friend, Karolyn Deans, who saw the typing of this manuscript as a way she could minister to me and to other women.

The endeavor has been a uniting of many people, as the apostle Paul said it should be.

Martha Hook

WELCOME TO EPHESIANS

You and the people in your study group are about to embark on an amazing trip through part of God's Word. You will be studying a personal letter from the apostle Paul. This letter is written to a group of friends that he valued highly and had spent long hours with. He loved this young church, cared for it, and at the time of the writing of the letter was separated from it. Why? He was in prison!

Why study Ephesians? This letter that Paul wrote as he sat in chains in Rome has become the jewel of the pastoral epistles (letters written to churches). Paul wrote to his Ephesian friends to encourage them, to teach them, and to answer some of their questions. Yet within the pages of this short letter are the keys to much of what has been used to guide the body of believers in the years since the letter was written. It has been said that all the rest of the New Testament theology will fit somewhere under the umbrella of the letter to the Ephesians.

Why study in a group? Since Ephesians was written to a group of people, not just to one person, it is ideally suited for a group study. This study guide will give you a framework on which to base your thoughts and a way to proceed through the teachings of this letter. This study divides each of the six chapters of Ephesians into two lessons; thus, there are twelve lessons. You will want to commit yourself to whatever time is necessary for your group to complete the twelve lessons.

Be careful. Sometimes a group starts with great enthusiasm and then dwindles or even dies from lack of interest. An honest assessment now of the time and effort required to complete the study will encourage you to "hang in there" when distractions come. Commitment is necessary and sometimes painful, but the rewards are worth it. God moves in response to our commitments!

The main benefits you will receive from knowing this portion of God's Word are the growth that will come to you personally as you study and the memory bank of God's wisdom that you will have stored up to draw on in the future. Do not forget, however, that you will be forming a bond of friendship with the people in your group. It may not seem possible when the group first starts out, but as you share concerns and insights, friendships will form. And the unity that Paul writes about in this letter to his friends will begin to happen right in the midst of your study group!

PREPARING FOR STUDY

You and your class are ready to begin. Exactly how do you proceed from here? A few guidelines may be helpful. Or you may want to set your own; be creative.

Most groups function best with a leader. Once you have formed a group, you may want to designate a person from within the class to assume the leadership; decide as a group who that person will be. Often the leader is the one who has formed the group and you will not have to decide on who the leader will be. The leader will help the class move smoothly through the material.

Some groups meet in different homes each week. The leadership of the group may shift each time you change the location of the study; the hostess for the day can be the leader for the day. But probably the best way for a group to function is to have the same leader for all the lessons. She will be prepared ahead to lead the class through the lesson and to stimulate discussion and sharing within the group.

Get Ready. This study guide assumes that you want to learn and study the Scriptures. Questions have been listed that will lead you through the Book of Ephesians. Real learning does not take place unless we earnestly apply ourselves. It will take time and effort to get ready for each session; set aside a time to study. Read through Ephesians at least once at one sitting before beginning this course in order to have the whole letter "in your head." Then, spend time studying the verses for the lesson in a more detailed way.

You will note blank spaces for you to answer each question. You should write out the answers to the questions before you meet with your group. If you will do this step in getting ready, then the class time can be spent in discussion and sharing rather than "just" answering the questions in a rote manner.

Remember that when you study the Bible, you will receive blessing in proportion to how much you put into the study. If you expect to get fed spiritually because the leader has studied, then you will and can learn. But you will miss those lessons God has prepared especially for you when you study the Scriptures on your own with Him. Who wants to miss out on that?

Can I study Ephesians by myself? Yes. This study guide will be helpful to you as you go through the book of Ephesians on your own. You may want to use this study guide as a devotional aid, or you may want to study Ephesians with the help this book provides. A "solo" trip through this letter can be rewarding. More information is given in the leader's guide for this series of lessons; it may be helpful to have the guide to refer to. You will find rewards for working through the questions and answers on your own!

SPECIFIC INSTRUCTIONS

1. *Set aside a time and place to study.*
2. *Ask God to help you as you study.*

3. *Read through the verses in the assignment.*

4. *Summarize the passage.* Briefly put in your own words what you think the verses mean; this is also known as paraphrasing.

5. *Note the "Key Verse" for each lesson and study it carefully.* At the end of each lesson, you will be asked to list a verse that has a special significance to you. Your favorite verse may or may not be the key verse.

6. *Work carefully on the last question.* This question asks what you have learned about God in the lesson. I think God will be looking over your shoulder in a special way as you answer this question!

7. *Make a note of any questions or problems you run into as you study.* Feel free to ask about these when your group meets; someone else probably has the same question.

WHAT MATERIALS WILL I NEED?

1. *Your own Bible in a modern translation.* I prefer one I can write in.

2. *A concordance.* Most study Bibles have their own concordance, but you may purchase one separately.

3. *A Bible dictionary or handbook.* This will give you a handy reference guide to use during your study time.

4. *A notebook for class notes.* Or be prepared to write in the study guide. You also may want to use a highlighting dry marker and whatever else will encourage you to be a good student.

A concordance and Bible dictionary will give you the beginnings of a good library of reference books about the Scripture. You will use them over and over again, not just for the study of Ephesians; consider them a good investment. Your own Bible, of course, is fine for this study. Extra purchases are not necessary. And the library in your church or city may have additional reference material you may want to use.

INTRODUCTION

As you read through the first verses of Ephesians, you will clearly see that God decided to love us before we were ever born. Long before creation, God was already at work deciding what He would accomplish on our behalf. The Scriptures, not just Ephesians, are an unfolding description of that plan. They are the record of God's loving intentions to restore us to our potential that was lost when sin entered the universe. Paul's letter to the Ephesian believers is a capsule in which he discusses God's love for them and how that love should mold their lives. As the Ephesians apply the truths that Paul writes about, their relationships—with each other and especially with God—are transformed.

Imagine this scenario: "Yesterday a close friend introduced me to his teenage son, and it was as if we always had been friends. We had a great visit. My friend had told me about this delightful but willful child of his before, but I hadn't met him until yesterday. However, before I met this boy I knew that I would like him and that someday we would be friends." All of us have probably heard or said words like these before. Our prior commitments and assumptions are important as we form new relationships.

Look at another example: Before our children arrive in our home, we parents commit ourselves to loving them, even though we don't know what their sex will be, what their abilities will allow, or even how they will look. Our preconceived determination assures our unborn children that we will care for them and love them. Of course, we can also think of times when the opposite reaction has unfortunately happened, and the parent will decide not to love and care for the child. The ensuing abuse and emotional destruction that will afflict such a child throughout his or her lifetime is always painful and often brings emotional illness—all because of a decision on the part of the parent before the child was born.

Just as these simple illustrations show us how earthly love among people can be influenced by preconceived commitments, so God's love is also based on what He decided about us before we were a reality. He loved us before the foundations of the earth, and He delights to respond to us as a result of that love. The understanding of this love is a transforming and foundational concept that new believers need to know about. Paul realized that the Ephesian believers needed to know what God's commitment to them could mean in their lives. Paul's letter speaks not only to the Ephesians, but it speaks to us as well. God loves us as He loved the Ephesians.

Read Ephesians as if Paul wrote the letter to *you*. It was written as a basic letter to believers and can be read personally, no matter who you are or what the date might be at the top of the letter.

The Backdrop for Ephesians

Every Greek city had three major areas, each with an elaborate building: a theater, a temple, and a sports arena. This was a result of the Greek insistence on training for the whole person. Ephesus, the city of the goddess Diana, was no different. All that is left of this city now, of course, is ruins, but the remains of these buildings remind us of the beauty that once was a part of the daily life of the Ephesians.

One of the main industries of Ephesus depended on the worship of the goddess Diana. The enormous temple for her worship dominated the city; it was one of the seven wonders of the ancient world. The temple was on the high point of the city. It overshadowed all of life and dominated a large percentage of the commerce of that time. Ephesus was like a tourist town, with souvenir booths everywhere. An entire industry of silversmiths had grown up near the temple in order to supply the demand for likenesses of Diana. You can imagine the fears of the silversmiths when people began to worship this new God, Jesus. Business began to fall off, and they got worried.

In addition to the following facts that will enrich your study of Ephesians, be sure to read Acts 18–20 to help you understand what was happening in the days of the early church at Ephesus.

1. *The emphasis on the male gender (Eph. 1).* The references to God as "Father" and the use of the masculine pronoun stood in sharp contrast to the worship of the feminine goddess, Diana.

2. *The description of Christ seated in the heavenlies and His appearance of prominence and dominance over all (1:20–22).* This image shows the risen deity of Christianity as an overpowering symbol in comparison to the lofty temple of Diana. The eyes of all the Ephesians would turn many times a

day to look up to the grandeur of Diana's temple; but in comparison to Christ's exaltation in the heavens, there is no contest. What a thrill it must have been for the Ephesians to then read: ". . . and seated us with Him in the heavenly realms, in Christ Jesus" (2:6).

3. *Paul's reference to the arrangement of the temple worship,* especially the ancient Jewish temple in Jerusalem (2:14ff.). The temple was built with two areas for worship: one was accessible only to the high priest and then only once in a while; the other was for the daily practices of the priesthood. The presence of God dwelt in the Holy of Holies, and the presence of the priest presided over the rest. The veil between the two was torn at the time of the crucifixion. Paul reflects on this fact of history to enrich the description of how Christ's peace with us enables us to be unified with one another.

4. *Paul's comparison of the temple with the body of Christ (2:18–22).* The cornerstone of any ancient building was of great significance and would usually be inscribed or marked in some way. This is the part of the building that archaeologists are always looking for to validate the date and importance of the building they are excavating. The picture of Jesus and His followers being a part of the dwelling place of God the Spirit would hold hundreds of mental pictures for the former worshipers of Diana.

5. *The reference to God as "one" (4:4–6).* This is a theme of the first three chapters, as Paul describes the deity of Christ and the worth of His place in the universe and in our lives. However, this was a radical departure from the kind of worship the Ephesians were used to. Their city believed in Diana, but they knew each city had its patron from among the list of pantheistic gods and goddesses. For the God of Christianity to abide as the unquestioned, solitary God of all was an important understanding for their young church to grasp.

6. *The sensual, dusky temple practices of the Ephesian pagans (4:17–19; 5:11–14) are set in contrast to the sensitive and moral worship of those who learn about and believe in Christ (4:20).* The use of the symbols of light and darkness would speak to the minds of the Ephesians, for they knew well what went on in the dark temple of Diana. Often the pagan worship of the gods and goddesses included temple prostitution and child sacrifice. To be able to speak openly with no shame or disgrace about worshiping Jesus must have given tremendous joy to this young church.

You may find other examples that will "flesh out" your understanding and help you see the Scriptures in three dimensions, not just on the page. The Ephesians were real people who lived in a real city and who bumped shoulders daily with a society of idol worshipers. Paul wanted them to see how the life of a Christian sharply contrasted to almost everything in their world. With an artist's attention to detail, Paul used visual and mental images from their community to draw his contrasts.

GENERAL OUTLINE OF EPHESIANS

ONE IN CHRIST

I. Basis for unity: What is it?
   A. God's eternal and individualized love package (1:1–23)
   B. God's complete forgiveness to both Jew and Gentile (2:1–22)
   C. God's expressed mystery to Paul and the Ephesians (3:1–21)
   Capsule of Ephesians 1–3: Paul's praise and expectations for Ephesian believers
II. Unity and Diversity: What's it all about?
   A. Explanation and results of unity and diversity (4:1–32)

B. How to live as part of God's family (5:1–6:9)

C. How to live in opposition to Satan (6:10–24)

Capsule of Ephesians 4–6: Paul's instructions and care for Ephesian family

ALTERNATE OUTLINE OF EPHESIANS
THE RELATIONSHIPS OF THE CHRISTIAN LIFE

Ephesians 1–2: Our relationship with God

Ephesians 3–4: Our relationships in the body of Christ

Ephesians 5–6a: Our relationships of the people of Christ

Ephesians 6: The enemy of the people of God

Purpose. These lessons are designed to help you study God's "how-to" manual on building unity with Him and one another. Ephesians shows God building His relationship with us and how He would have each of us build relationships with one another. The format of each lesson will include questions to help you understand the assigned verses in Ephesians, questions on parallel passages to help develop your awareness of this epistle, and questions for discussion and application of the lesson to today's life. As you study with your group, you may find that the principles of Ephesians will begin to develop in the showcase of the class. By the end of the study, all group members should be able to see how God has taught them principles and how they have been able to put the theoretical into practice within the loving concern of the class.

Goal. "And be kind to one another, tender-hearted, forgiving each other, just as God in Christ also has forgiven you. Therefore, be imitators of God, as beloved children; and walk in love, just as Christ also loved you, and gave Himself up for us, an offering and a sacrifice to God as a fragrant aroma" (Eph. 4:32–5:2 NASB).

YES, JESUS LOVES ME

Ephesians 1

No central problem in the city of Ephesus caused Paul to write this letter; rather, he wanted the Ephesians to know and realize what God was doing in the church. Our heavenly Father's goal in the coming ages is to show forth His grace by revealing what He has done through His salvation in our lives.

This letter has become the capstone of Paul's theology because it provides an overview into which all of Paul's other writings fit. In the beginning of the letter, Paul discusses the work of the Godhead in providing for our salvation. The Father planned it, the Son accomplished it, and the Spirit then applies it and becomes its seal.

Paul then writes down what he has been praying about for the Ephesians. He is thankful for their love and faith and asks that God will give them open hearts. If this prayer is answered, then they will understand their calling, inheritance, and especially God's power toward His people. This sort of growth makes unity a natural outgrowth of God at work in the lives of His children.

1

GOD'S WORK IN SALVATION

Ephesians 1:1–14

Key Verse: "In love he predestined us to be adopted as sons through Jesus Christ, in accordance with his pleasure and will" (1:5).

THE BASIS FOR UNITY: WHAT IS IT?

The amazing nature and depth of God's love for us is made clear in the beginning of Paul's letter to his beloved Ephesians. God's infinite love is not a haphazard afterthought, nor is it a love based on compulsion; rather, His love has caused Him to act in a methodical planning for my interests before I even came into existence. It is not a small plan, but a grand and gracious scenario, masterminded and executed for my benefit by all three persons of the Godhead. The plan is "a deal I can't refuse," and it's without price tag or hidden costs. God's love for us is based on His unconditional love for the human race.

Summary: Put Ephesians 1:1–14 in your own words.

_____

_____

_____

_____

_____

STUDY QUESTIONS

1. Read Ephesians 1:1–14. Make a list of the things with which God has blessed you. Note the tense of the verbs in these verses. How do you react to this, and what does it tell you?

_____

_____

_____

_____

_____

_____

_____

2. How has God chosen to "see" you (1:1–14)? How do you choose to see people? Next, name three people and describe how you have chosen to see them.

_____

_____

_____

_____

_____

_____

_____

3. What does it mean that God lavishes forgiveness on you (1:7−8)? _____

_____

_____

4. What gift would you give to show that you love someone? How has God done this for us (1:13−15)?

_____

_____

_____

_____

5. What is the work of the Trinity described in this passage (1:1−14)? _____

_____

_____

_____

6. What does this passage tell you about God?

_____

_____

_____

_____

7. What verse in Ephesians 1:1–14 is most meaningful to you? Why? _____

_____

_____

_____

_____

_____

Questions I want to ask about Ephesians 1:1–14 when our class meets next:

1. _____

2. _____

3. _____

4. _____

2

PAUL'S PRAYER FOR SPIRITUAL AWARENESS

Ephesians 1:15–23

Key Verse: "I pray also that the eyes of your heart may be enlightened in order that you may know the hope to which he has called you, the riches of his glorious inheritance in the saints, and his incomparably great power for us who believe" (1:18–19a).

Paul's prayer for the Ephesians is a wonderful insight into what his expectations were for this group of young believers. It is his personal prayer list of things that only a Christian would want. It is also a song of praise about what God has done for us, a "hymn to the risen Christ." Paul, like many preachers at the end of their sermons, "prays home" what he has just finished saying to them in verses 1–14. He hopes that the realities of God's love will become as basic to the Ephesian church members as the realities are to him as he writes from prison. Finally, as he prays that they might become more aware of what Christ has done for them, his prayer turns to praise for God's work shown in what Christ has accomplished. Paul closes this prayer with praise for Jesus' place in heaven today.

Summary: Put Ephesians 1:15–23 in your own words.

_____

_____

_____

_____

_____

STUDY QUESTIONS

1. Why does Paul give thanks for the believers in Ephesus (1:1–15)? _____

_____

_____

_____

_____

_____

2. What does Paul pray for as he remembers his friends (1:15–18)? _____

_____

_____

_____

_____

_____

_____

3. Read Acts 18–20. Knowing what you now know about Ephesus and how Paul was treated there, how would you have prayed for the church at Ephesus?

_____

_____

_____

4. What is taught about God the Father in this passage (1:17–20)? _____

_____

_____

_____

_____

5. What is taught about Jesus Christ in these verses (1:20–23)? Why is this description of Jesus so vital to the Ephesians' understanding (Acts 19:27–35)?

_____

_____

_____

_____

6. In your opinion, have "the eyes of your heart" been opened to Jesus? How? Do you feel you have a grasp on His love for you and what it means (1:17–19)?

_____

_____

_____

_____

_____

_____

7. What does this passage tell you about God?

_____

_____

_____

_____

8. What verse in Ephesians 1:15–23 is most meaningful to you? Why? _____

_____

_____

_____

_____

Questions I want to ask about Ephesians 1:15–23 when our class meets next:

1. _____

2. _____

3. _____

4. _____

TRUTHS TO REMEMBER FROM EPHESIANS 1

1. God's eternal plan and care for us.

2. The work of the Trinity in our lives.

3. The themes of God's sovereignty and human choice.

4. The hymn to the risen Christ.

PROPERTY OF
BROADWAY CHRISTIAN CHURCH LIBRARY
910 BROADWAY
FORT WAYNE, IN 46802

A HOUSE UNDIVIDED

Ephesians 2

In Ephesians 2, Paul describes God's work to bring us into His family. While we were dead in sin and living under the rule of Satan, God made us alive in Him because He loved us unconditionally. And He raised us to a new position. We are seated with Christ in heavenly places. This is an expression of His grace. We did not deserve it, but we were saved because of His abundant love (2:8–9).

The amazing result of God's love and grace is that this new position is available to both Jew and Gentile alike. It also makes Jew and Gentile one in the family of God. This oneness breaks down all the barriers between us and paves the way for the unity in God's family. The earthly standards of perfection that divide people are no longer valid. No longer do the old rules show who is the best or the favorite, for God has brought peace rather than performance to rule in all of our relationships.

Access to His presence rather than alienation from Him is now our privilege. We have become partners in the same household where God dwells through the Holy Spirit. Our physical bodies now can house His presence, and we can have fellowship with believers from all backgrounds.

3

THE MACHINERY OF GRACE: HOW DOES IT WORK?

Ephesians 2:1–10

Key Verse: "But because of his great love for us, God, who is rich in mercy, made us alive with Christ even when we were dead in transgressions—it is by grace you have been saved" (2:4–5).

Ephesians 2 begins with a reminder of what the Ephesians had been like before they discovered the gospel. They were under complete control of their wicked society, unable to free themselves from its power over their lives and thinking. The contrast is obvious. From reading the first part of Paul's letter, you already know what it means to be a part of God's plan. Now Paul wants to be sure that we remember what our former life was all about. We were controlled by sin and by the "ruler of the kingdom of the air" (2:2). We are never to forget God's grace in springing the trap of the hold that this world's system had upon us. Nor do we want to forget our former status in contrast to our current position as part of God's unified family.

Summary: Put Ephesians 2:1–10 in your own words.

_____

_____

_____

_____

_____

STUDY QUESTIONS

1. Whom is Paul describing in 2:1–3?

_____

_____

_____

2. What does it mean to be "dead in trespasses and sins" (2:1 and Rom. 5:8)? _____

_____

_____

_____

_____

3. How aware of the "ruler of the kingdom of the air" were the Ephesians (2:2)? How are you aware of him (Acts 19:11–19 and 1 Peter 5:8–9)? _____

_____

_____

_____

_____

4. Read Ephesians 2:1−5 and Romans 3:23. Complete the following paragraph by filling in the blanks with your answers: "It is _____ to see that I am a sinner. I am most conscious of it when _____ _____. My normal reaction to this awareness is to _____ _____."

5. Imagine what the scene described in 2:6−7 would look like with you in it. Write out your description and your reaction to it. _____

_____

_____

_____

_____

_____

_____

6. What did "saved by grace through faith" mean to the Ephesians (2:8)? to the Jews? What does it mean to you?

_____

_____

_____

_____

7. What does this passage tell you about God?

_____

_____

_____

_____

8. What verse in Ephesians 2:1–10 is most meaningful to you? Why? _____

_____

_____

_____

_____

_____

Questions I want to ask about Ephesians 2:1–10 when our class meets next:

   1. _____

   2. _____

   3. _____

   4. _____

4

GRACE + PEACE = UNITY OF BELIEVERS

Ephesians 2:11–22

Key Verse: "But now in Christ Jesus you who once were far away have been brought near through the blood of Christ" (2:13).

If unity of the believers is the theme of Paul's letter to Ephesus, then this lesson describes the crucible of how it can happen. Unity is only possible when the basis for it is Jesus. Paul describes this unity both in theory and in symbol. Those who were "far off" (anyone who was not Jewish, specifically the Gentiles) are brought "close" by Christ's blood. Now we tread on the same argument that caused the Jews of Christ's time to say, "Crucify Him!" The Jews had ostracized all who did not practice their religion and its laws. Paul introduces the shocking new principle that Jews and Gentiles will share in worship. Next, Paul explains symbolically how all believers are built into a spiritual temple. The cornerstone is Jesus, the foundation is the wise people of the faith, and the building is the believers. We are together in Jesus and are a temple for the presence of God.

Summary: Put Ephesians 2:11−22 in your own words.

_____

_____

_____

_____

_____

STUDY QUESTIONS

1. How does the Gentile differ from the Jew (2:12−13)?

_____

_____

_____

_____

_____

2. What has Jesus done about these differences (2:13−22)? How does this affect you? _____

_____

_____

_____

_____

3. What type of a building is described in this passage (2:19—22)? _____

_____

_____

_____

4. Read Exodus 40 and Ephesians 2:14—22. How does the old temple compare with the new?

_____

_____

_____

_____

5. What is the "barrier" Paul mentions (2:14)?

_____

_____

_____

6. Is there unity between you and your friends? Take one difficult relationship and discuss your struggle with unity.

_____

_____

_____

_____

7. What does this passage tell you about God?

_____

_____

_____

8. What verse in Ephesians 2:11—22 is most meaningful to you? Why? _____

_____

_____

_____

_____

Questions I want to ask about Ephesians 3:1—13 when our class meets next:

1. _____

2. _____

3. _____

4. _____

TRUTHS TO REMEMBER FROM EPHESIANS 2

1. All are saved from sin through faith.

2. The unity of the Jew and Gentile.

3. The temple of the true God is built from believers.

4. Jesus is the Cornerstone.

A SECRET TO BE TOLD

Ephesians 3

Paul wants the Ephesians to know about a special concept that God has revealed to him. He calls this concept a "mystery." Since no one had anticipated the fact that God would unify the Jew and the non-Jew in the Messiah, Paul wants to be sure that the believers in this Greek outpost understand this new idea. And not just the idea, but the reality of what it means in life. The unifying of the Jew and the Gentile is the distinctive message of Paul's ministry. God had not revealed this message before, and now it is Paul's privilege to herald it.

While many think that the body of believers is the weakest and most disorganized institution in all of history, Paul states that this amazing confederacy is a tribute to God. It demonstrates God's power to transform enemies into brothers and sisters. This mystery is taught and discussed among the rulers in the heavens because even the aangels apparently had no prior understanding of this concept. What seems weak and divided on the surface is the witness for all time to God's grace and wisdom.

Paul, who is overwhelmed by his privilege as the "keeper" of this new revelation, prays that we may begin to fathom what is the greatness of God—an awareness that surpasses all human knowledge or understanding. When we look at the alienation in this world and realize what God has done to make us one, we begin to get a new comprehension of God's grace. It is truly "immeasurably more than all we ask or imagine" (3:20).

Be sure to notice that this chapter is a parenthesis between Ephesians 2 and 4. As Paul begins to talk to the Ephesians about their lifestyle, he seems overcome by the awareness of his mission, a mission that has led him to prison. He takes this part of the letter to share with these new believers his attitude about what God has called him to do. He refers to himself as a prisoner in 3:1, then seems determined to prove that it is a privilege, not a problem, to be in prison as a result of such a high calling. After this explanation, he continues his original intent of discussing how Christians should live.

5

PAUL'S BLUE-RIBBON PARENTHESIS

Ephesians 3:1–13

Key Verse: "In him and through faith in him we may approach God with freedom and confidence" (3:12).

Paul, by his own description, was the least of all saints, and it is hard for him to believe God has honored him by giving him a ministry. This surprises us because we know history recognizes Paul's tremendous influence. However, try to understand Paul in his first-century context. To the Christians he was the former Jewish zealot, who was now in prison for the very faith he used to violently oppose. Many probably still feared him. The non-Christian sector saw Paul as a troublemaker, a political problem, and a religious fanatic.

Three topics with striking implications are highlighted in this part of Paul's letter: 1) The Jew and the Gentile are co-heirs of the blessing of God through Jesus; 2) Paul's changed life and resulting ministry had an incredible impact; and 3)

God uses the body of believers to present Himself to the world.

Summary: Put Ephesians 3:1—13 in your own words.

_____

_____

_____

_____

_____

STUDY QUESTIONS

1. Why does Paul interrupt his prayer in verse 1?

_____

_____

_____

2. What is Paul's opinion of himself as a minister of the gospel of Jesus Christ (3:1—13)? What is your opinion of yourself? Explain. How does Isaiah 1:18 apply to you? to Paul?

_____

_____

_____

_____

_____

_____

3. What is the specific mystery Paul has been shown (3:3—11)? _____

_____

_____

_____

4. The stories of Stephen and Paul are entwined in the New Testament. How do their stories meet and compare in Acts 7:51–8:1 and Ephesians 3:8–13?

_____

_____

_____

_____

_____

_____

5. Why is the encouragement to boldness and confidence necessary for the church at Ephesus (3:12)? What part does fear play in your daily routine? _____

_____

_____

_____

_____

_____

6. What does this passage tell you about God?

_____

_____

_____

_____

7. What verse in Ephesians 3:1−13 is most meaningful to you? Why? _____

_____

_____

_____

_____

_____

Questions I want to ask about Ephesians 3:1−13 when our class meets next:

  1. _____

  2. _____

  3. _____

  4. _____

6

PAUL'S FAMILY PRAYER

Ephesians 3:14–21

Key Verse: "And I pray that you . . . may have power, together with all the saints, to grasp how wide and long and high and deep is the love of Christ" (3:17–18).

Do you ever pray for someone you really love? Often those prayers reveal the depth of your caring, for you seek God's highest for those you love the most. Paul's prayer for his newly hatched brood of believers shows us how much he cares for them. He prays that God will enrich their lives and cause them to stand firm. At the heart of Paul's prayer is a desire for the Ephesians to realize who Jesus truly is and how much He loves them. If they develop their knowledge of Jesus, their growth will naturally follow.

This prayer brings to a close the theological section of Paul's letter. He will move on into the more relational topics in the next chapter; however, this first section, Ephesians 1–3, is the foundation for all unity and growth. Paul tells us that no one succeeds at being a Christian without Christ in control of his or her life.

Summary: Put Ephesians 3:14–21 in your own words.

_____

_____

_____

_____

_____

STUDY QUESTIONS

1. What "reason" is Paul thinking of in 3:1 and 3:14 (see Eph. 2)? _____

_____

_____

_____

2. Why does Paul mention the family so often in his prayer? Do you have a friend who is like family to you? Describe how this category of friend fits into Paul's world and yours.

_____

_____

_____

_____

_____

_____

_____

_____

3. What does it mean to be strengthened in the "inner being"? Compare 3:16 with 2 Corinthians 4:8–18.

_____

_____

_____

_____

4. How do you fit into Paul's prayer list (3:15, 18, 21)?

_____

_____

_____

_____

5. If you have struggled with human love, what does 3:17–19 mean to you?

_____

_____

_____

_____

_____

6. What does this passage tell you about God?

_____

_____

_____

_____

7. What verse in Ephesians 3:14–21 is most meaningful to you? Why? _____

_____

_____

_____

_____

_____

Questions I want to ask about Ephesians 3:14–21 when our class meets next:

1. _____

2. _____

3. _____

4. _____

TRUTHS TO REMEMBER FROM EPHESIANS 3

1. Paul's parenthesis about his ministry.

2. The three miracles:

   a. Unity of the Jew and Gentile.

   b. Paul's changed life.

   c. God's use of the church.

3. Paul's prayer for the Ephesians.

THE NECESSITY OF UNITY AND DIVERSITY

Ephesians 4

UNITY AND DIVERSITY: WHAT'S IT ALL ABOUT?

Paul explains to the Ephesians about living as believers on the basis of God's love and grace to all mankind. He first emphasizes the unity of the believers, but it is not quite so simple. Paul is equally concerned that we understand God's delight in diversity. The key to being a mature believer and living at peace with those around us is found as we learn to balance the tension between unity and diversity.

The cultic worship of the Ephesians had formerly dominated their lives with its sensuality and idolatry. But now Jesus has given them new principles of dealing with their own emotions and of living honestly with those around them. The difference between the hardened heart of the unbelieving person in Ephesus and the tender heart of the new Ephesian Christian is the basis for attaining unity within the body of Christ.

This part of Paul's letter teaches us much about the need to keep unity fresh and growing within the church. How is this possible? The main vehicle for accomplishing this growing unity is to understand that we each have a different function in the body of believers. This allows us the supportive love of those around us while we are enjoying the freedom of living out our own unique category of service. And all the while we are worshiping and praising God together for what He has done for us.

7

WALKING WORTHILY

Ephesians 4:1–16

Key Verse: "Instead, speaking the truth in love, we will in all things grow up into him who is the head, that is, Christ" (4:15).

Paul's letter has thoroughly explored the foundation of our faith and the riches of God's love. Now, Paul explains how we can live on the basis of what he has taught us in Ephesians 1–3. These next three chapters are practical and personal; they will teach us about walking with the changed outlook of this new life.

One of the most quizzical truths of God and His plans for us in this world is: How can God use both unity and diversity in harmony? We want everything to fit into our categories, and we want to define the categories. Paul first shows us seven unities that belong to all believers: one body, one Spirit, one Lord, one faith, one baptism, and one God and Father. On these God wants us to build our growing faith.

Then he explains that we each have been given a different way to serve God. We have both the security of the unity and the personal identity of the diversity.

Summary: Put Ephesians 4:1–16 in your own words.

_____

_____

_____

_____

_____

STUDY QUESTIONS

1. Make a list of what we need to "live a life worthy of the calling" we have received (4:1–3).

_____

_____

_____

_____

_____

2. Why does unity require so much hard work (4:3–6)?

_____

_____

_____

3. How do you perceive unity and diversity in the church today? How is your church like Paul's description in 4:4–13?

_____

_____

_____

_____

_____

_____

_____

4. How are unity and maturity related (4:13−16)? How do you rank your own maturity level? Has it changed recently? Why or why not? When are we grown up?

_____

_____

_____

_____

_____

_____

5. What part of the body are you? What are your gifts and role in life? Think of two people and explain how you perceive their place in the body. (Choose two from the class if possible.) _____

_____

_____

_____

_____

_____

_____

_____

6. What is the source of our differences (4:8–11)?

_____

_____

_____

_____

7. What does this passage tell you about God?

_____

_____

_____

_____

8. What verse in Ephesians 4:1–16 is most meaningful to you? Why? _____

_____

_____

_____

_____

Questions I want to ask about Ephesians 4:1–16 when our class meets next:

1. _____

2. _____

3. _____

4. _____

8

AN AFFAIR OF THE HEART

Ephesians 4:17–32

Key Verse: "You were taught . . . to be made new in the attitude of your minds; and to put on the new self, created to be like God in true righteousness and holiness" (4:22–24).

Paul uses some forceful language in writing to the Ephesians, who are beginning to try to live as followers of light instead of darkness. He says things like "I insist" and "you must quit." Activities in their pagan culture ran counter to living with unity from the heart, and Paul wants the Ephesians to understand the serious nature of learning how to live as a believer.

We begin our Christian walk with faith in Jesus, but parts of our growth will come only with fierce determination to set aside the old ways and to put on the new. In setting aside the old and putting on the new, we begin to grow from the inside out. Once our heart is captured by God's love, our lifestyle can change. Our affair of the heart with God is now making unity with those around us a pleasant possibility.

Summary: Put Ephesians 4:17–32 in your own words.

_____

_____

_____

_____

_____

STUDY QUESTIONS

1. Contrast the condition of the heart described in 4:18 with that described in 4:32. _____

_____

_____

_____

_____

2. What does it mean to you to have Paul insist that you change your lifestyle (4:17, 21–24)?

_____

_____

_____

3. Describe the heart attitude and actions of the Gentiles (4:17–19). _____

_____

_____

_____

_____

_____

4. What three-step process does Paul suggest (4:22–24)?

_____

_____

_____

_____

5. How can we defeat the Devil (4:25–27; Matt. 4:1–10; James 4:7)? How can you put these ideas into practice?

_____

_____

_____

_____

_____

_____

6. Paul writes like a general giving orders in a battle. What orders does he give (4:25–32)? _____

_____

_____

_____

_____

7. What difference will following Paul's orders make in your heart? What difference will it make in the sense of unity you desire with those around you?

_____

_____

_____

_____

8. What does this passage tell you about God?

_____

_____

_____

_____

9. What verse in Ephesians 4:17–32 is most meaningful to you? Why? _____

_____

_____

_____

_____

_____

Questions I want to ask about Ephesians 4:17–32 when our class meets next:

1. _____

2. _____

3. _____

4. _____

TRUTHS TO REMEMBER FROM EPHESIANS 4

1. Unity and diversity must be in balance.

2. The seven unities.

3. Truth is God's viewpoint.

4. Gifted people help the church grow.

5. We must put on the new style of life.

6. Emotions are okay; sin is not!

HOW TO LIVE AS PART OF GOD'S FAMILY

Ephesians 5

Paul encourages us to be living illustrations of the One whom we worship. If we live like this, we will be transformed in all parts of our behavior—our actions, our motives, and our words. The difference in lifestyle between the believer and the nonbeliever is similar to the contrast between light and darkness. As believers we can be called "children of light."

As this process of maturing continues, the influence of God's will and Spirit becomes more pervasive and more powerful. The result of this continual process of growth within us is a thankful heart. Our life becomes a song of praise to God and an expression of our thanksgiving.

Paul gives the Ephesians principles for the home that are vastly different from those principles that guided their former lives. The new believers want to imitate God in their family relationships. A serving heart and attitude should characterize the members of a Christian family, and each family member is given simple yet powerful guidelines to accomplish this goal. Mutual submission within the home is the pebble dropped into the pond of life. The ripples that spread out in ever-increasing circles splash into all areas of home life. Paul highlights the marriage relationship first. The husband and wife are specifically guided to live together with a quality of love similar to Christ's love for the church. This chapter not only explores the marriage relationship but also sets the tone for Ephesians 6, which will explore other relationships within the family.

Unity at the level of the family is often the most difficult to exercise, even though it is the unity we most want and need. Without this sense of unity and the security it provides, parents and children struggle with imbalance in the other areas of life. The resulting family problems are woven into our emotions and hearts; constructive family life is equally powerful and much more desirable. Paul's instructions recognize that if we are "imitators of Christ," we will love and care for those around us, especially those in our home. We will have a new sensitivity and attitude of caring about each individual.

9

LIVING AND LOVING IN LIGHT

Ephesians 5:1−21

Key Verse: "Be imitators of God, therefore, as dearly loved children and live a life of love, just as Christ loved us and gave himself up for us as a fragrant offering and sacrifice to God" (5:1−2).

In these first verses of Ephesians 5, we are encouraged to walk on a light-filled path and to treat one another in love and concern; Paul says we can do this because "we are all members of one body" (4:25). Paul encourages us to love and care for our family in Christ. We all function together to form that spiritual corporation that Paul calls "the body of Christ."

Paul gives us another checklist in 5:3−7. If we are imitating God and loving one another as a result, our sexual responses will be kept within their proper framework; our material possessions will be owned with thanksgiving, not greed; our conversations will be based on integrity, not emptiness. With these guidelines in mind, we are to be determined to be a partner in the family of God, not a partner with the idolatrous or the disobedient. Paul then encourages the Ephesians to "submit to one another out of reverence for Christ" (5:21).

Before studying this lesson, re-read the last verses of Ephesians 4.

Summary: Put Ephesians 5:1–21 in your own words.

_____

_____

_____

_____

_____

STUDY QUESTIONS

1. What does it mean to walk in love (5:1–2, 8, 15)?

_____

_____

_____

_____

2. What references to the Ephesians' idol worship are tucked away in 5:1–12 (see Rom. 1:20–25)?

_____

_____

_____

_____

_____

_____

3. Explain Paul's use of the symbols of light and dark (5:8–14). What parallel do you see in our culture today?

_____

_____

_____

_____

4. Why does Paul insist on understanding the will of God and what pleases Him (5:17; 1 Thess. 4:3–8)?

_____

_____

_____

_____

5. What two kinds of "filling" are compared in 5:18–20? Why? _____

_____

_____

_____

_____

6. Verse 21 sets the stage for the rest of the letter. Think about its implications. What is your reaction, and how can you live it out? _____

_____

_____

_____

_____

_____

_____

7. What does this passage tell you about God?

_____

_____

_____

_____

8. What verse in Ephesians 5:1–21 is most meaningful to you? Why? _____

_____

_____

_____

_____

_____

Questions I want to ask about Ephesians 5:1–21 when our class meets next:

1. _____

2. _____

3. _____

4. _____

10

LIVING AND LOVING AT HOME

Ephesians 5:22–33

Key Verse: "However, each one of you also must love his wife as he loves himself, and the wife must respect her husband" (5:33).

Built on Paul's insights about service and submission to one another, this lesson gives us specific guidelines for a healthy and lasting marriage. This gets our attention, for even with all our books, counselors, and seminars on marriage, our society constantly struggles to find success in the partnership that is supposed to be for life.

Paul turns his spotlight to relating, and he then isolates the area that gives each person the most struggle. For the woman, this problem area is to live under the leadership of her husband. For the man, this area is to consistently love his wife. The keys to solving these problem areas are found in the wife's respect for her husband and in the husband's committed love for his wife. Simplistic? Perhaps one thinks so until each suggestion is put to the test. Then we realize that Paul's wisdom for the Ephesian homes reaches into our contemporary lifestyle with ever-fresh advice.

Summary: Put Ephesians 5:22–33 in your own words.

_____

_____

_____

_____

_____

STUDY QUESTIONS

1. Review the ten basics for living as believers (4:1–5:2).

a. 4:1–2 _____

_____

b. 4:3 _____

_____

c. 4:15 _____

_____

d. 4:22–23 _____

_____

e. 4:25 _____

_____

f. 4:26 _____

_____

g. 4:29 _____

_____

h. 4:31 _____

_____

i. 4:32 _____

_____

j. 5:1−2 _____

_____

2. What will happen if we put these new "Ten Command-
ments" into practice at home? _____

_____

_____

_____

3. What are Paul's instructions to wives (5:22−24, 33)?

_____

_____

_____

_____

4. What are Paul's instructions to husbands (5:25−30, 33)?

_____

_____

_____

_____

5. Explain Paul's illustration in 5:23−33 and how it applies
to you. _____

_____

_____

_____

_____

6. What is the original recipe for a marriage (5:31; Gen. 2:24)? How does this recipe apply to marriages today? What do you see as the controlling factors in today's marriages?

_____

_____

_____

_____

_____

_____

_____

7. What does this passage tell you about God? _____

_____

_____

_____

_____

8. What verse in Ephesians 5:22–33 is most meaningful to you? Why? _____

_____

_____

_____

_____

_____

Questions I want to ask about Ephesians 5:22–33 when our class meets next:

1. _____

2. _____

3. _____

4. _____

TRUTHS TO REMEMBER FROM EPHESIANS 5

1. Imitate God's love.

2. Reject darkness.

3. Live in light.

4. Submit to one another.

5. Wives, respect your husbands.

6. Husbands, love your wives.

FIGHT THE RIGHT FIGHT

Ephesians 6

The instructions for a godly home life are extended to children and servants in this chapter. The knowledge that all are equal in God's eyes will encourage masters and servants alike to serve God in all they do. This should be the attitude of all family members. They are not to war among themselves, but to love and serve one another.

On the other hand the believer is to take the dualism in this world, that continual struggle between good and evil, very seriously. This is where to fight! And Paul's instructions carefully prepare us for that battle with the evil powers of the universe. Paul likens our readiness to fight against evil to a soldier putting on his armor before battle. Each piece of the believer's suit of armor not only helps us in our fight against Satanic forces, but also helps us in our attempts to maintain unity in our relationships.

Implicit in this lesson is the fact that some Christians do not realistically admit they will have battles in the Christian life. "Christians are people of peace and joy," they say. We are, but we must also be prepared when Satan tries to destroy our unity, peace, and joy.

Paul prays for protection and encouragement for all the saints as well as for himself. The letter ends with Paul's prayer for grace and peace for the Ephesian believers.

The contents of this letter were never intended for the eyes of believers thousands of miles from Ephesus and two thousand years later; Paul's letter, however, does give us consistent and contemporary information about the joys and struggles of the unified life of the believer. Remember, if Paul had not been in prison, neither we nor the Ephesians would ever have had this letter. Thus we can be thankful for our "ambassador in chains." His words in Ephesians 3:13 become very personal: "Do not be discouraged because of my sufferings for you, which are your glory."

11

LIVING AND LOVING AT HOME— THERE'S MORE

Ephesians 6:1–9

Key Verse: "Serve wholeheartedly, as if you were serving the Lord, not men, because you know that the Lord will reward everyone for whatever good he does, whether he is slave or free" (6:7–8).

How can we live together in harmony? Paul now addresses the children and those who work in the home. Paul first focuses on the most difficult area for children: obedience. He reminds them what the law of Moses said about obedient children; they are promised a good and long life. This is simple advice, but the living out of Paul's wisdom is not as easy—ask any child! Parents, too, are challenged to live with their children in harmony, not in an atmosphere of constant criticism and friction.

The slave and the master are encouraged to cheerfully serve God, who is the true master of both. Our goal as believers is to be responsible workers and respected overseers.

Summary: Put Ephesians 6:1–9 in your own words.

_____

_____

_____

_____

_____

STUDY QUESTIONS

1. Notice Paul's different uses of the term "children [sons, infants]" (1:5; 2:3 [KJV]; 4:14; 5:1, 8; 6:1). As you are a growing person in the Lord, explain where you are now in your spiritual growth. Infancy? Childhood? Adolescence? Adulthood? _____

_____

_____

_____

_____

_____

2. Is there ever a time when we can disregard our family ties (6:1–3)? Explain. _____

_____

_____

_____

3. What psychological tips for healthy family life are found in 6:1–4? Briefly describe yourself in childhood and adulthood. If you have been a parent, also describe yourself in that role. _____ _____

_____

_____

_____

_____

_____

_____

4. The Ephesians lived in a two-class society: slave and master. Apply 6:5–9 to our day.

Employee: _____

_____

_____

Employer: _____

_____

_____

5. What basic principles do you find for service in 6:5–6? How do you plan to put them into use?

_____

_____

_____

_____

6. What "equalizers" are given as we try to unify relationships within the family (5:1; 5:21; 6:8; 6:9)?

_____

_____

_____

_____

7. What does this passage tell you about God?

_____

_____

_____

_____

8. What verse in Ephesians 6:1–9 is most meaningful to you? Why? _____

_____

_____

_____

_____

Questions I want to ask about Ephesians 6:1–9 when our class meets next:

1. _____

2. _____

3. _____

4. _____

12

PREPARE TO PROTECT UNITY

Ephesians 6:10–24

Key Verse: "Therefore put on the full armor of God, so that when the day of evil comes, you may be able to stand your ground, and after you have done everything, to stand" (6:13).

The letter ends with Paul's loving salutation. As if taking a deep breath, he gives some good but tough advice. He wants the Ephesians and all of us to know that a war is going on in the spiritual realm. It affects everyone. So Paul gives some guidelines for doing battle against evil.

Paul makes it clear who the true enemy is. It is not self; I am a child of the King (1:5). It is not another Christian; we are unified into the body of Christ (2:19). It is not my family; we are servants of God and each other (5:12). Our enemy is Satan, who wants us to fight one another and our God. Our unity would then be destroyed. Paul warns us to be ready for the right battle with the right equipment and to prepare ourselves through prayer. To keep the faith and its unity, we must constantly be on "red alert" with a prayerful attitude before God.

Summary: Put Ephesians 6:10—24 in your own words.

_____

_____

_____

_____

STUDY QUESTIONS

1. What fact does Paul assume? Note the tense of the verbs in 6:11—12. _____

_____

_____

2. Describe how we should defend ourselves (6:10—17). Did Paul forget about our back? _____

_____

_____

_____

3. What results can we expect if we follow these instructions (6:10—17)? _____

_____

_____

_____

4. What two inner defenses does Paul recommend (6:18—20)? For which does he ask for himself?

_____

_____

_____

5. What was the last purpose of Paul's letter (6:21–22)? What does this tell you about Paul?

_____

_____

_____

6. What is Paul's last request for the believers in Ephesus (6:23–24)? Contrast 6:23–24 with 6:10–17.

_____

_____

_____

7. What does this passage tell you about God?

_____

_____

_____

_____

8. What verse in Ephesians 6:10–24 is most meaningful to you? Why? _____

_____

_____

_____

Questions I want to ask about Ephesians 6:10–24 when our class meets next:

   1. _____

2. _____

3. _____

4. _____

TRUTHS TO REMEMBER FROM EPHESIANS 6

1. Children, honor your parents.

2. Fathers, do not antagonize.

3. Servants and masters, serve God first.

4. Stand firm against Satan.

5. Use God's armor and *pray*.

IN CLOSING

I hope the beauty of this letter by the prisoner, Paul, has become yours. This short piece of Scripture is a masterpiece of logic and love, woven together in a message for us today. Practice it! Possess it! The message will never wear out and can continue to refresh your spiritual growth throughout your life. Allow God to use Ephesians in your life as a practical tool for growth and service. And use it to stay close to those around you. "Unity" is not a clinical term, but a message from God about communion and commUNITY.